The Blinking Anthology

Edited by Samantha Rose

ISBN: 978-1-4716-0191-0

www.blinking-cursor.co.uk

Contents

Editor's Note

Thank you for buying or downloading this book, which is brought to you by Blinking Cursor Literary Magazine, which is brought to you by myself and all of the great writers who have contributed. I started Blinking Cursor in 2009 and the first issue was what I now like to think of as a beta – there were grammar mistakes I hadn't picked up on, I was charging for downloads which seemed to turn people away somewhat, and I had accidentally put the page numbers on the wrong corners!

The second issue came out much better and by then the magazine had also gained more interest. It has only gotten better since then, which is why I decided that it would be great to be able to release something a little bigger, and so the Blinking Anthology came about. It has taken a little longer than anticipated, with me recently getting a full time job that I really enjoy, but there will always be time for Blinking Cursor.

So I would really just like to thank all of the writers who over the past eight issues (at time of print) have submitted their work for publication in BC, and Adrian Jamison, who created the BC logo, Jim Fuess whose artwork has appeared on many covers of the magazine, and of course you, the reader, for taking an interest and sticking with us over the past three years. It's not always easy being a one man band, but it is definitely fun and made even better by all of you. So thank you very much for reading, and here's to the next three years.

Harlequins

As harlequins in the wind
Your laugh flies with me.
It envelops me and rises in mid-autumn,
Makes me grow and mature in silence.
Maybe it grows dark for some
But, my love, only your love is enough for me
To reach eternal paradise in life,
To be able to daydream of your eyes,
And so to forget, amongst all, those tears.

By Gonzalo Salesky

Handwriting On the Wall

They say it makes no sense to teach longhand,
instead the young use keyboards for their text.
Pen and paper now remote as quill and stand,
technology is what the writer's voice directs.

And I myself put all my thoughts on screen,
where once they lived between a pad's blue lines,
but all the years and changes that I've seen
cannot obscure the penmanship once mine.

Those hours passed in sweeping loops and slants,
sole letters linked as words enscorceling,
a hope that something beautiful might chance
to be revealed when mute desire learns to sing.

And though the page is now a glowing screen
the writer still must scribe what it will mean.

By Jerry Kraft

Quick Come Quick Go
(for Yi Ming)

in haste
you came
on one of those
dull or desperate days
like a summer shower
catching me in the open
without an umbrella:
my heart swept afar
my soul rain-drenched
and my bored body
left standing alone
among isolating pools
as you leave
in a hurry too

By Changming Yuan

The Move

The room and I did not choose each other:
Circumstances have shipwrecked me here
In this shaped vacancy which seems
Geometrically indifferent to my needs,
Uncomfortable as new shoes. Reluctantly
I unpack, stick posters on walls, the banners
Of an occupying army. Now I must wait
As if to be rescued. In time, the room
Will contain friends, be warm on winter nights,
Acceptably surround me as the radio sings
Of possible relationships. By the time I leave
This space will be a perfect fit for me.

By David Whippman

Flying

All you catch of dolphins from shore
are their fins,
thin slices of black
that cut through the top layer
of the water's crust.

Although the other day
I saw one
whole,
atop a cresting wave.
He flew,
like a surfer,
before he plunged back into
the crack of the invisible.

By Ruth Gooley

Bakersfield Star

Have you ever been to Bakersfield? Most people just stop to pee there. Lana lived in Bakersfield.

Before Bakersfield, Lana lived in Tengiz, Kazakhstan. In case you've never heard about it, it was in the middle of nowhere. There were tumbleweeds, camels, and oil. There were also Americans looking for oil.

Lana dyed her hair like Marilyn Monroe, powdered her freckles with lilac-scented powder, and wore midnight-blue eyeliner and stop-sign red lipstick. She sang sad Russian pop-songs and dreamed of being a movie star as she served whisky and vodka at an oilfield bar. At twenty two, Lana got sick of camels and tumbleweeds and married an American safety manager, John. He was tall, with a square jaw and brick-red hair and always wore a plaid shirt.

John gave Lana a diamond ring and took her to Bakersfield. Bakersfield is in the middle of nowhere. There are no tumbleweeds or camels there. There are a lot of Americans. Tons of oil. Starbucks. Costco. And that's it.

In nine months she had a baby boy with brick-red hair. Then she had another baby boy, then another, all three bubbly, plump and with brick-red hair.

And so the years went by, and Lana lived in a five bedroom house with carpeted floors and a swimming pool she never swam in. She baked her own bagels. She gained weight. During the day she chopped onions for lasagna, made chicken soup and cheese cakes, vacuumed the beige carpet and loaded the washer with the boys' jeans and plaid shirts.

Sometimes she got all dreamy and put detergent in the chicken soup. Sometimes she locked herself out of the house and sat in the dark garage and cried in the car, her forehead on the wheel, the boys asleep in the back seat. Sometimes she talked on the phone with her neighbor Jackie while ironing jeans and plaid shirts. Lots of jeans. Lots of plaid shirts. Or she watched Oprah and cried. And then she baked more bagels—cinnamon, sesame and garlic. Every night she sang good night songs to the boys and then sat by the window, staring at an exhausted birch-tree by the pool and drinking vodka.

"Listen," she whispered to the birch-tree. "Listen, every day I hope that not today, but maybe tomorrow I will wake up different."

Every morning she would wake up sweating in her flannel pajamas, bags under her eyes. She'd put on her jeans, size 16, and make-up to cover sun spots on her cheeks, pull her unwashed hair in a ponytail, and put the empty vodka bottle in the trash.

Every birthday John gave Lana a golden ring from Costco in a small red velvet box and took her out for drinks. Each time Lana drank a cranberry vodka. Then she drank one more. After six vodkas, she would turn to him and say, "This is it?!"

"What do you mean," her husband would answer.

"That's life?!"

"Stop screaming," her husband would say. "People're looking."

"Let them look. I don't give a damn!"

John was a really good guy. He loved Lana. He knew that next she would jump on the bar and start stripping, just as she used to do in Kazakhstan when he first met her and she was a size 0, her hair was soft and sunny and she looked like Marilyn Monroe. He would gently pull her outside where it smelled like cow shit.

And every year Lana would look up, and high in the skies she would see bright cold stars twinkling at her—better than diamonds on her fingers, better than vodka in her glass. She had seen them in Kazakhstan. There they were, full of magic, fairy tales, wonders and lies. They still promised, they still whispered about miracles and faraway lands with no sun spots, no laundry, no Costco. No tumbleweeds. No bagels. No oil.

The stars knew everything so far was a mistake; they knew there ought to be more in life for her.

By Zarina Zabrisky

Emancipated Innocence

As Spring came to an end
I locked away my inner child
at the bequest
of anticipatory adulthood

and embraced the heat of Summer
with my so-called maturity
far too busy to enjoy
the warmth of the sun

It took Autumn's fleeting beauty
to help me understand
that our most precious seasons
are all too brief

Thankfully the coming winter
frees the child within me
and together we try on old mittens
in hopes that heavy snow is on its way

By Alan D Harris

Dandelion Shine

Nina sits on the grass in front of the white house with the black roof and adds another flower to those in her hands. They are bright yellow, warm as sunshine, tiny tiny petals layering against one another to make their solid-looking blossoms. Those blossoms she has pressed together, adding each one at a time. They form a perfect sphere, like she's captured the sun to give it to her mother.

The stems are full milk, and when she picks a new flower - snap - it dribbles out onto her chubby fingers. They stick to the stems, to themselves, and to her pink shorts as she tries to wipe them off.

The sun is high overhead, almost lunchtime, and heat waves shimmer above the asphalt when Nina stands and stretches her legs. She presses her nose to the edge of the sphere and sniffs. The tiny petals tickle, and when she looks up again there is a smudge of yellow on her sunburnt nose. Her right hand clenches around the cracking stems, so many she almost needs two hands to hold them all.

But she needs her other hand to get into the house. As it is, of the three doors she can only open one, not tall enough for the others. Nina holds the flowers and watches them as she takes one step, then another, toward the side of the white house with the black roof.

Shade covers her as she steps around the corner, as cool as walking through the door to the mall. The worn boards of the old fence are to her right, flowers growing up under them through the space in the pavement. The house is on the left, the side door halfway down, but she doesn't look at it. She's still admiring the sunshine warmth of the flowers, imagining how her mother will smile.

The buzzing noise starts somewhere near the far corner of the house. Nina stops walking and looks over the fence with wide eyes until she sees it. A fat bee searching the flowers, weaving an unsteady path from one to the other.

"Does it hurt?" she'd asked her brother not even a month before, looking at the angry red welt on his arm.

"More than a needle," he'd answered, leaning forward to share it like a secret. "And the bee dies, rips its guts out and leaves them behind in your arm."

Now her arms shiver in the cold shade, the striped T-shirt she'd put on in the morning offering no protection. She watches the bee move from flower to flower and then looks at the sphere of yellow in her hand, so close to her bare arms.

The sliding door, so easy to open, is around the back, past the bee. It opens from the porch and onto the dining room by the kitchen where her mother is washing dishes, unable to see any flowers.

Stems crack again as she tightens her fist and looks at the side door. She's grown some, a new mark on the wall at her last birthday. The bee is still far away.

Nina runs. Her canvas sneakers tap against the pavement until she reaches the door and stretches her hand up to the handle.

She can reach it. The metal is cold against her skin, especially compared to her mother's flowers, still clenched in her other hand. She pulls the door.

It rattles against the frame, but does not open. Nina looks up, sees the button above the handle. Remembers her father holding her up to try it once.

"You have to push the button in. Don't worry, you'll get it when you're bigger."

She's bigger now, but the button is still too high. She glances over her shoulder.

The bee is coming toward her.

Nina whimpers, stands on her tip toes, feels her side stretch and pull as she reaches for the button. She can feel the curve of the edge against her fingertips, but she still can't reach and the bee is right behind her now.

She drops the sphere of flowers and runs. The buzzing stays behind her as she clamours up the steps of the deck. The sliding door opens with a whoosh, closes with a thud.

"Nina?" Her mother is standing by the sink, suds up to her elbows. She leans back to look at her daughter who has her face pressed against the glass door, yellow-smudged sunburnt nose all squished up. "What's wrong?"

Nina doesn't answer.

She waits a week for the bee to be gone, refuses to walk past the side of the house the whole time. When she's finally certain it's safe the flowers under the fence are seed-puff balls, more like snowflakes than sunshine.

There is no noise in the shade, buzzing or otherwise, as she creeps up to the side door. When she reaches it, she kneels down. The flowers are still there, the perfect sphere flattened to a perfect circle. Her mother's capture sunshine, abandoned as she fled, faded into brown mulch and grey dust on the pavement.

By BD Wilson

Blue

I cannot look on the bright side
When it's set below the horizon

Subjecting me to perpetual darkness
With nothing but pin points of light

Maintaining their distance
While the moon acts as a mirror

Reflecting what I no longer feel
While leaving me cold and blue

By Anthony Ward

damn.

all I have to do is keep going
and really, how difficult could that be?
well, we'll see.
all I have to do is put one word after another
my fingers do all the work
all I have to do is sit there and let it happen
but when it doesn't happen
and when it's not so simple
I drag it around with me everywhere
and it's heavy.
so I look around and wonder
what now?
how do these things work?
where do I begin?

jesus christ.

I could be rolling a cigarette in the shade
on some sprawling tree-lined campus
watching the girls walk by talking
about this weekend or the last,
sitting in the back row watching the clock,
opening a beer back at my place
then another,
brilliant, all-in and generally
not giving a damn
but open to
everything.

keep going.

a single light in the shattered dark
ashtray bottles in a grinning window
some pearl-snap bastard shoves me at the party
dead drunk stumbling walk back to the building
three in the morning
they all go home with their catches
and skin each other alive on the chopping blocks
the mattress springs uncoil and tear through
music in the next room slaughters the walls
red-eye dead-eye
sleep like cinder blocks
when the morning
breaks screaming.

the sound would've stuck with me

I would've been someone else completely
too many variations to count
any time or place.

the alarm goes off.

By Austen Roye

Death's Doorway

Keratinous,
the fingernails of the old man,
Yellow and discolored,
too much nicotine absorbed through the years,

Wind and weather browning and hardening his skin,
as if the mummification process begun,
while he still breathed,

The smell in the room,
one of death or dying,

The eyes serene,
the life lived evidentially a good life,
but where is his kin,
a shame no one here to see him off,

only me, an intruder,
come only to find a doctor or nurse,
for my ailing son,
I smile down,
he slowly nods,
and closes his eyes.

By Douglas Polk

Exodus

By the end of each shift at Niles Market, the boy tired of
getting yelled at by the assistant manager to gather carts
scattered all over the parking lot, an endeavor invariably
leaving somebody's gum, spit out at any random spot
on the summer asphalt, stuck to the treads of his shoes
(he might as well have dodged dog crap in the park,
which at least has green grass on which to walk barefoot)
or to more quickly pack the groceries into paper bags,
which he already did so well, so rectilinearly, that the full
bags could be used as bricks for the foundational layers
of a pyramid, just as well as he stacked the piles of fifty-
pound fertilizer bags kept in front of the fourth and fifth
cash registers; everyone wearied of Fargo's bullying and
sourceless bitterness, from the blue-smocked, bleached-
blonde cashiers to the thick-armed, public-school stockers
to the other baggers, youngest and lowest on the totem pole
but forced nonetheless to wear bow ties, shitty clip-ons,
and white shirts buttoned all the way up, despite heat,
despite the need for a little slack, so the boy whispered
here and there, and they all left, each from their stations,
some having the presence of mind to grab want ads from
the papers in the rack by the automatic doors, some having
stolen whole quartered chickens, bags of chips, ice cream,
cases of beer and pop, all driving off to the park by the lake
for an impromptu store barbecue like the one the recent bosses,
the management, promised but never delivered each summer.

By John F. Buckley

Salsa de Archimedes

A man steps out of a cab he wasn't
in and it becomes the season when

I was you, well, not exactly, but I wore
your shoes and thought myself a lady,

when childhood was a hummingbird
unaware he had wings, or a bottle of

vintage bubble bath in a tub with a drain
that didn't stop, and we didn't stop,

not one of us, not when the twisting
arpeggios of the flamenco's hands

taught us how to spell our mothers' faces
and how to place them in the back of our

throats where they wouldn't come out, not
even for a shout of *Eureka!* from the bath.

By Karlanna M. Lewis

Her Name is Angel

A cliché.
When she shakes
the loose hair
from her pillow
after her third round,
she's tired but still
not unique.
Some days, she sits
at the toilet for hours
because it's easier
that way and she rests
her warm face on the cold
of the white tub.
She looks for her camera
to record the soccer games
of her children
with the heart shaped faces.
She, along with everyone
else is unsure.
Her hair grows back black,
with circles of gray at the top, like halos.

By Heather Wyatt

The Woman at Redondo Pier

Ancient but timeless, a woman suspected
mad holds audience with our sane glares.

Around her waist, above a green skirt, she's
tied bright sweaters – an archive of colors.

Before they can be asked, boardwalk vendors
hand her free cupfuls of hot or cold liquids.

She totters along the pier, pausing at boat slips –
this woman miswandered from Joyce's Dublin.

Her neck a crooked arch, she rolls a cigarette,
head oddly canted as if peering down a staircase.

As gulls glide through each other's shadows,
she wears that stiff smile only the manic know.

The overcast sky feints a promise of sunlight.
She speaks to no one visible, and we all listen.

By Jeffrey C. Alfier

Evening

Bath
full

our
bodies

            tumble
release

            tumble
release

wringing
out

the dryness
of another day.

By Kristina England

Last Autumn

Amazing how many stars
fit inside my windowpane.

A flying carpet of
sugar maple leaves
unfurls along my road.

Just enough light to glimpse
silhouettes of yellow trees
against the dove grey sky.

Tenacious…one ragged
leaf clings to the bough.

After evening showers,
a garden of bright meteors
blossoms.

Stopping to see the
shape of a snowflake.

By Joan McNerney

Meadow's End

Wander with the spirits,
Entreat a blossom bloomed,
Step, trip, side step,
Welcome, breathe, the humid gloom.

Boughs twisted into terror,
Deformed witches with long reach,
With hair of leaves and smells so sweet,
Who shivers in the wind and creaks.

A path of muddy blood and veins,
Pounded, dusted, collecting bones,
Gather around grave leather boots,
Amid roots deep, deep in their throes.

The sturdy path straight curves from view,
Away, far away, too far to see,
In the gloom, the gloom, lost to eyes,
Too heavy, too dark, to bear crow's scream.

A shift, a twitch, damp in the mist,
To the side, to the other, to above, to forever,
Echo, echo, echo, from the sides,
So distant, so crude, too cleverly near.

Follow the path, dare walk the curve,
A light amidst glints off skin, too bright,
They'll see – who's they? – doesn't matter, they will,
They're lurking, they're waiting, for a moment right.

Step forward, step forth, the meadow closes,
Great beasts of bark and wings of flowers,
So tall, so wide a path, too devilishly near,
The meadow's end draws forth its final power.

The spirits wander ahead of you.

By S. R. Christian

Impact

It's how we found each other dancing
on railroad tracks with pennies

in our pockets, pieces of dreams
decaying in caves beneath our skin

shadows from bordering trees trembling
under our feet, our bodies so young

this forest was a kind of ghost
story we weren't afraid of anymore

the thunder of a locomotive whistle
so loud our ears pulsed like hearts

our hands reaching into our pockets
finding what they feel like empty

because we forgot our mothers
can't afford pockets without holes

the train coming closer towards us
the growing light, an angry finger

pointing at us, with quivering hands
we run to pick up the fallen

pennies scattered along the tracks
the ground shaking with purpose

our fingers wrapping themselves
around pieces of copper, the dead

of night looming, the train light
piercing the nerves in our eyes

our fists full of pennies, the screaming
whistle sounding louder and louder

one by one we lay them down

By Mercedes Lucero

The Spinning Globe of My Mind

For the first time in five years
I sit here at my desk
in the exploratory realm
where I doodled for imagination.
I notice the walls absent
of thumbtack holes
and pencil markings
recently touched up
by my father's handiwork.

The slow sloth years of a teen
spent in minutes upon hours
staring down my reflection
in glass-cut concentration
of what it was I had to do.

At my left a globe
I spun frequently while waiting
for a shakedown of an idea.
On my right was a small lamp
which would hypnotize me
to the grid in my mind.
I would then adjust the direction
of light onto the white space
of the wall with my profile
mapped out like the globe
losing its circumference.

Now with my legs cramped
at the knees under this desk
where I did more visioning
than accomplishing my homework.
In the midst of this poem
where home is a long lost
friend and those unknown friends
within the travels yet to make
that I write from
the landscapes of my mind.

By Michael Berton

Cocktails

The lobby shone like a rat trap
all angles and metal corners,
waiting for a bit of weight,
a step in the wrong direction.
The lost, drooping flowers
spit their petal to the anaemic floor
and dangled off pots swinging from the ceiling.
It all looked muscular and angry.
The air itself a tight fist
that refused to give.
The crowd trailed in
with grins clinging to their faces,
eyes reflecting the bars,
the metal, the snapping hinge.

By Valentina Cano

Melancholy

Somebody cut off the tongue
of my loneliness

your eyes look like scrambled
eggs

nobody
blinks

no mirrors
in between.

I use the gas to toast my love
and
the butcher's knife to spread
the butter.

By Peycho Kanev

I Never Saw Anyone Actually

wear one of the sweaters my Aunt Minna made.
We thanked her, praised her, held up whichever one
we got. Held it against ourselves, showing off
the argyle crew neck or raglan-sleeve cardigan,

too heavy for the slim framed, too flimsy for the broad.
And to boot, the colors, oh the colors she picked to knit
-- mostly shades of off-green and puce, and all sale yarn,
at that. Yarn that rendered her colorblind

to our skin tones, heedless of our body shapes. Content
with and bent on fashioning the correct size garment
with unreasonable color and texture, she knitted on
and on, her bone needles click-clacked their way to

the end of each row of sale yearn, each garment growing
less and less into what we needed, wanted. Her efforts,
though collectively rewarding her with love
and attention, thwarted any request for

further sweaters, let alone hats, scarves or gloves, so,
she turned to crocheting -- crocheting more sale yearn
into a carton full of four inch squares she fabricated into
one afghan, after another. That handiwork

was later followed by neon pom-pom tassels for tying
on luggage, which allowed her to use up every last bit
of leftover yarn in her possession. To this day, those
eye-popping beauties adorn suitcases of mine that ride

round airport carousels, sit in train-station baggage
claims, stand amid a throng of travelers
anywhere, anytime. And each time
I eye one, I smile.

By Ruth Sabath Rosenthal

Walking Backwards

I would walk backwards across the room
just to keep you in sight, just to hold your
swimming eyes against the pale plate
of your miraculous face. I would stumble
over chairs for you, put my frail dignity at
risk. Overcautious until I met you, I would
leap from the roof into an eight oz. water
glass. I would sign a release, risk that
delicious fall and squeeze, the wet and
cold and broken glass and shattered
bones, I would, I would fly in a formation
of bats, I would sing my guts out on TV.
This is the promise I make, the vow if you
will, the seal of my irrevocable desire.
Even as you recede from me and windows
open their cavernous maws, I will walk
and walk backwards into oblivion – memory
and myth like an inkblot, an irremovable stain.

By Steve Klepetar

The Professor

Every day he walks
bony bare ankles
too short pants
dress shoes, hair as if
he electrocuted himself
looking not right
not left
not at the cars
stopped for his
wiry frame.
Elbows perched at his sides
like chicken wings
like prehistoric body parts
he walks
his mission:
find the water
hear the waves
drink the coffee
read two pages
maybe three
of prose carried
in his back pocket
or the baggy pocket
of his cardigan sweater
always black
over dress shirts
short sleeved
one pocket on his
concave chest
perched glasses
bothering his perspective
occasionally he trips
or falls off curbs
he thinks it is
payment for a small
life. Where he has
one pre-prepared salad
in his fridge
a quart of milk and
tea, although he
walks to coffee.
He loves the girl
at his morning stop
she must be 20
just starting out
still living at home
he wants to hold her
he wants to kiss her
he wants to adopt her
he does not know

what he wants except
to see her, except
on Wednesdays
he does not know
what she does Wednesdays
but still he goes
he must be consistent
he must get his
exercise
he must matter.

By Tobi Cogswell

new year's day

at this point, I have let slip
the parameters of the acceptable;
I know only the fragility
of the soul and how it stuns
the senses and pierces the lead
of civility; that I am here
for a short span and must cling
like dew to the sympathetic
arms of my kind: you who touch
me not with your fingers and see
my form not with your eyes;
above those who view me
as commodity, as a means
to an end, a novelty of a time
intended to be shortlived;
above those tied by blood
and gene; rather, I live
for those that walk beside me
in thought and discernment,
who ask nothing and take nothing
and in doing so give everything -
for these very ones are the guardians
of the art of my life; we are hunters
all: seekers of truth as well as love -
I won't be reluctant in my review
of you, be it fond, feverish or vexed;
at some point you will hear
from my mouth every thought,
act and response to you before
this journey winds to its pause,
and I warn it will be sooner
rather than later - as now,
from this moment,
I am quite unbolted

By Amanda Anastasi

Why I love the moon

I love her best when I catch her
dreaming her private dreams,
aloof, a distant Buddha

far enough to tempt to fancy
near enough to cast her anchor
hard in our hearts.

We adore her, poised against endless night
magnet to immensities
beyond us.

By Janet Butler

Confessions of a Retiree at Christmas
(in memory of Jack Micheline)

Funny how skin folds in on itself,
A limp canvas over muscle and bone.
My wedding band's stuck

Behind the second knuckle.
I nibble on trail mix
As my Greyhound moans to Vegas.

A tumbleweed rolls through the crosswalk.
Venus appears over a mesa.
We enter the Land of Driveways:

Children barefoot the asphalt
Watching father string lights
Under the eave of their roof.

Mother's at the door hanging a wreath.
I weep behind a moonlit window
While stars dance the Zodiac sky.

By Kirby Wright

Whispers

Out there among the trees,
way down at Santubong
the whispers in the breeze,
bring back an ancient song.

Way down at Santubong
sad sounds of long ago
bring back an ancient song
a song the spirits know.

Sad sounds of long ago
the whispers in the breeze.
A song the spirits know,
out there among the trees.

By Colin W. Campbell

Clean and Fresh Things

The Paganellis were a nice family, you might agree. Mr. Paganelli was married to his wife for 19 years after all. He worked in stocks and had lost a lot with the economy down. But his family still attended the block barbeques and his wife still wore the prettiest dresses and made the best blueberry-lemon cobbler—so they can't be too bad off, their neighbors thought. But at the turn of winter, the Paganellis began to decline their dinner party invitations. Everyone suspected Mr. Paganelli's money was thinning, so most could understand if the family was less social, and even the Paganelli's closest friends didn't inquire very much. Yet they did not know, for Mr. Paganelli was vehement that no one know, you see—none knew about the infestation.

You might argue it affected Mr. Paganelli the most. The bugs left their greatest marks on him, penny-sized bites—the result of a bad reaction to them, his doctor said. They itched and burned throughout the day. In the privacy of his office he would hold his phone with one hand and scratch with the other as he watched the market drop on his computer. Telling his wife about his day, he would often scratch his arms in between sentences, not noticing that he was until he looked down and saw the marks of his untrimmed nails across flushed skin. Hiding it wasn't easy. One silent night, he—the exterminator—showed up in front of the house in an unmarked van as requested, and a jolly dog of sniffed out the haunts of the creeping things. It took two visits from the exterminator before Mr. Paganelli and the dog were both satisfied. He had the beds thrown out, mattresses and bed frames included, as well as the couches and bean bag his daughter had since childhood. If anyone asked—the wife's redecorating, he would say. Until the new mattresses were delivered, they all slept on the artificial ones he bought, the kind of ones filled with hot air. Floating on one, he had the worst of his nightmares, dreaming he had become one of the bugs himself.

But though he was quite tormented, you might say the whole affair left Mrs. Paganelli the worse off. After all, it was she who had first discovered one crawling across her violet quilt which went so well with the rosewood bed frame. And though she loved her bed very much, she couldn't hide her happiness when it was thrown away and she began searching for a new bed set—the perfect excuse, she thought. She bought nothing used. However, you could not expect Mrs. Paganelli to part with her clothes. These she had to wash in hot water herself because she had fired the maid—God knows what filthy things that woman was bringing into the house. Afterwards, before she put any of her things on she would sneak into the bathroom with it. There, with a fierce lurching she would shake her blouse over the clawed bathtub, hoping for any lurking bug to drop onto the cold white surface. She observed every fell piece of lint with the greatest suspicion. Once, she actually found one of the awful things, in her husband's suit pocket of all places, and she pressed her thumb against it until it burst and died and she calmly urged it down the drain, keeping the discovery to herself. She could not wash several items—her fur coats and delicate beaded dresses; these she threw in knotted trash bags to be stored in the basement. She would have to wait three months before she could be sure anything unwanted in them had died and she could reopen them. Until then, she bought several new dresses and coats. And when she had heard from a neighbor that the Bonrick's had bedbugs she shook her head and remarked what an awful thing to happen to such good friends.

And still you might think their daughter Jill suffered the most. She was only in high school and unequipped to handle such a domestic travesty. Imagine applying to college with that hanging over you. She certainly stopped going to the movie theater—they're in the seats, I heard! And when she visited friends she was conscious of their furniture, avoiding the beds of others as a rule of thumb. When she heard they could crawl into books she stopped visiting the public library—better to get them new. And she was the most upset by the cancelled vacation—those hotel beds, her mother argued. Indeed, it must have been hard on her.

But once the infestation was finally eradicated, they became a considerably happy family again for at least a year or two. Though the market was swinging, Mr. Paganelli was doing well enough, and returned to giving the best financial advice over dinners. Mrs. Paganelli forgot all about the bags in the basement, and when she did remember she decided the clothes in them were out of fashion anyway and she threw them out unopened. Their daughter Jill went to a nice college a long way off. All in all they seemed quite unblemished. It was therefore a thrilling shock to their neighbors and friends when, on the eve of the anniversary, Mr. Paganelli took his own life in his closet. The funeral was well-attended and dreadful—but he was so secure, they whispered—especially for Jill, who beforehand had to endure the sounds of her mother shaking her new black dress over the tub, whipping it so that in her hands it became a cape, as if she were saying: Come! I dare you—come! And it wasn't until she was back in college and she had washed her white sheets that Jill cried properly, mourning what an awfully clean and fresh thing her bed was as loud music played somewhere in her dormitory.

By Samuel Diaz

Thoughts About the Dispossessed

A strong yearning to go home
and this awful weather signals
red to me, like the traffic police
of fortune and desires.

My feet, restive with brimful
vigour irritates my peace.
Cold winds add tumult
and thoughts clutch
as sweat of humidity.

Heavy head and paining eyes
paste me to bed and
jog my memory
of those who sit
without desires in roads,
dispossessed with frayed rags.

The report card of their whims
have been torn by the all-pervading.
and scattered to places far away
from their vision,
too remote from their reach.

My days will get over
with the Sun spearing the
flowing clouds but
they are marked as spots
raising finger at civilization.

By Dr. Sonnet Mondal

The quiet room

You wince under the waits' added load.
Squashed seating arrangements anticipate
breasts squeezed into scanners.
We are blind to fresh flowers, pastel curtains and carpets.
Receptionists and nurses maintain the default cheeriness
of shopping channel presenters but
fear runs amok amongst us
strangling our instinct to chat.
The pages of 'Hello' are turned with shaking hands,
eyes skim bikini clad celebs,
whilst we strain for a bustling nurse to pop her head
around the door and sing your name.
A girl in Sainsbury's uniform nuzzles
her boyfriend's shoulder.
It must be confusing for men,
this switch from 'Carry On' fondling to
reluctantly tracing a lump insidious as an IED.
Afterwards, we watch other women liberated by
'Every thing's fine you can go'
But for one woman, the nurse in sotto voce voice,
'Would you come through to the quiet room?'
My eyes meet yours,
we remember boxes of tissues and the private exit.
15 minutes trudge by.
'For God's sake'
You re-cross legs, switching your coat about you,
I sit with every muscle clenched.
Discharged suddenly, we scurry from the building, high on relief.
I slam the car door on the nurse with the valium voice
and her open invitation for me to join her in 'that room'.

By Fiona Sinclair

So Long at the Fair

It was going to be a trip home that Johnny already wanted to forget.

"Well, did you have fun today?" Veronica asked him, clearly not amused.

"Why, didn't you?" Johnny asked, sensing tension in the air but uncertain about what had brought it on this time.

"Seatbelts have a purpose. Intend to use them?" she asked, louder than before.

Working at the county fair didn't appeal to him at first, but Veronica used a kiss and nudge to charm him. He'd man the beer tent, and she'd cut the ladies' cakes and pies for the lunch crowd at Jaycees Hall.

Sunny and hot in August, you needed a beer to cool down at the counter between opening bottles of Star . . . the brew that made Iowa famous. The hog cooler at the Pack was the place to be today, he thought. But then he remembered what it was like to leave the plant in this heat . . . like walking into an oven. After twenty-two years, he still couldn't get used to it. So, a Star tasted darn good. Grease kept his black hair in place. He wiped the sweat with his forearm.

"Hiya, Mike," Johnny said, putting on his grin. "How are the guys?" He added a double-barrel belly laugh, and Mike shook his head, smiled, and walked on.

Next, he saw Brenda and her beauty mark. "Well, look who's here! Ole Johnny," she said, walking up to the bar with a sashay. "Can you open one for me, honey?"

The sun shot in Johnny's face, bringing him back to reality. Seatbelts. He dug underneath the cushion and clicked the silver buckle in place. "Alright, the seatbelt's on. Satisfied?" he asked.

"Pull it tight," Veronica snapped. The broad band wrapped across his waist tightly. There was heat but no air inside the Studebaker. He put it in gear and they bounced over the grass in the open-field parking lot.

"Good thing we're leaving now before the supper crowd comes," he said, turning to Veronica and attempting a grin. She pulled down the visor to cut the sun and glanced at the dash often. The car slid over the grass, and he let out a laugh.

"Johnny, be careful."

"I'm fine."

"What are you doing?"

"Trying to get home. OK with you?" Why did it always have to be like this? he wondered.

They paused at the fairground exit, and when the coast was clear, Johnny nudged the car forward onto two-lane County EE.

"Just take your time!" she insisted.

"Really, Veronica, I'm fine."

He banged his hand on the steering wheel, and the sedan jerked as he lifted his foot off the brake and then sharply back on again.

"Was that necessary?" she asked in a huff.

"Listen, I'm only trying to get us home."

"Acting like a schoolboy trying to impress his buddies."

"So, I had a drink."

"A drink?"

"Yes!" Now he was the one with the voice. "So what? I had a drink."

"I saw you at the tent. Handing out bottles like they were lemonade. One for him, two for you."

"I had a drink."

The automatic feature was new on the Studebaker, and all he had to do was add pressure to the gas. She sped along the road as sweet as you please. He fiddled with the right knob and heard Chubby Checker singing for a moment before she turned it off.

"No distractions," she mouthed. "Focus on the road. And why are you taking this road?"

"To get home. What is this? Fifty questions?"

"I'd like to get home a-l-i-v-e," she snapped, giving a two-syllable word at least five. "Careful, the speed limit is 55."

"Going 50."

She let out a sigh and looked straight at him.

"You're drunk!"

"I said I had a beer."

"I can smell it on your breath. I saw what you did. You were drinking and you're drunk."

"Look, I'm not your father. You don't have to worry. I had a beer. Is that a crime? I can see there's no point talking to you."

"You're pathetic," she said.

"One beer makes me drunk?"

"It wasn't just one beer. I saw you."

"So, you saw me grab a beer. That makes me drunk?"

"Don't deny it. What I saw, I saw."

"What did you see?"

"I saw you down it like lemonade. Then, you opened a bottle for Brenda! Disgusting."

"Oh, so that's it!"

"I know what you see when you're drunk."

He tightened his grip on the wheel. Just then, a black roadster sped down the S curve. Johnny piled on the brakes and saw the other driver's eerie face.

The Jaycees thought this year's fair attendance was among the best. Some of the supper crowd were delayed by an accident and detour on the county road.

By Jan Wiezorek

Vignettes From A Postcard Town

A railroad bum
With two watches
On the same wrist
Swings beaten-up drumsticks
Through the air
Though there isn't any music

At the post office
Where Market meets Hayes,
A speed freak
Smelling like stale tobacco
And an obvious transient
Who has the strong odor
Of inexpensive wine
Escaping from her pores
Wait in line
To mail letters
Going nowhere

Every Sunday night,
The old Asian women
Rummage through trash cans
For recycling gold
Because Monday morning
Is trash day

At 9 AM,
An impatient drunk
Waits by the front door
Of a bar until it opens,
But doesn't realize
There's another one
Up the block
That's been serving drunks
Since 6 AM

A green toilet
Sits by itself
On the sidewalk
And everyone who passes by
Wonders if anyone has used it,
But nobody has the guts to look

By Michael N. Thompson

Black Hats and Black Ties

It must be twenty years
since I last saw her,
wisps of blond hair
sailing from her black hat.
I wait until the last grain of earth
bounces from the coffin lid
before I go over to her.
I smile, she frowns
and I know that my memories
are not hers and I step back
but this time just to tie up
the laces of my shoes.

By Idris Caffrey

The Cat

shadows run and play
as the world wakes up
trees unfold their leaves
a cat climbs an oak
impales it with little cat feet
leaves its mark
in the meaty soul of the tree

a world of nature
the sun
the shine
the blue
grey skies
left behind

the unclouded hand
of God knows
when to laugh
when to cry
just as the cat knows
when to run
when to play
all day
alive and free
up his tree

By William D. Hicks

Confinement

Commander Jones had thought it would be easy, a planetary smash and grab. They would land two dozen heavily-armed warbirds on Bernelli 7, and grab the cache of rare minerals known to exist there. The whole thing should take only a week, Earth time. It seemed easy enough.

"Commander, it looks like they have finished walling us in," said his second-in-command, Sgt. Clare.

"I can see that, Sargent. So there have been no more attacks, just them building that wall?"

"That is correct, sir. The air seems okay, at least. And there is water here," Sgt. Clare finished.

"Looks like they want to keep us alive. Sargent, make sure the troops sequester some rifles somewhere. Bury them, whatever.

"Roger that, sir. Anything else I should tell the troops?"

"Just to get started on some kind of shelters. Just because those damned bugs live in holes, does not mean we have to."

Jones had thought that the heavier proton beams would shred the strange barrier. But they merely went through it. Whatever the alien creatures were using to erect it, Earth weapons were ineffective. Soon, the humans had been herded into this godforsaken crevice by tens of thousands of Bernellians, armed with simpler projectile weapons - too many of them. The Earth forces were defeated, and had to surrender - a concept the Bernellians understood, fortunately.

He looked at the barrier, shimmering in the distance. It rested on a natural rise of land, around three kilometers long and a couple wide, their best guess. The Buglike creatures were spraying some kind of substance on a latticework made of energy beams. In some ways these creatures were way behind Earth tech; not in this way! The humans would have to sit tight, regroup, and think of another strategy.

Cmndr Jones walked back into a larger encampment, ringed with some remaining proton weapons.

"Where is my science advisor? I need to talk to her!"

A tall woman in uniform ran up. "Right here, sir!"

"Advisor...Eliason. It seems to me we have to prepare to be here a while," said Jones.

"That much is obvious, Sir. Nothing will get in or out of that Barrier. But there is ample water supply here, and fertile land. So we are not without recourse, even strategic recourse."

"Okay, then. So they left us in a place where we can plant crops, grow food, drink. A nice place for a colony." Jones looked at her directly.

"Exactly, Sir. They could have wiped us out - but instead chose to confine us. Like they want to study us."

Cmdr Jones said nothing for a moment. Then;

"You said strategic recourse. Meaning what?"

"Well, plant material can be distilled to extract volatile oils, flammable materials. We merely have to see what kinds are growing here. We may be able to build a dirty explosive, and have a go at the Barrier that way."

Jones scratched his dirty hair. He felt the weariness of lack of sleep, and constant stress. Taking some deep breaths, he continued:

"Alright. You are tasked with forming a study group. The goal is construction of bombs to attack the Barrier. You can also make sure our long-range transmitter is hidden - perhaps it can be repaired so we can call for help. If a Bug team comes looking, they should not be able to find these things. Understood, Advisor?"

"Understood, sir. I'll get right on it." She strode off, shouting orders to others along the way.

Commander Jones was speaking with some fellow soldiers, when a group of the Bernellians came calling. Two were waving their tentacles high in the air, holding white bits of material.

The universal sign of parley. all right, here goes then.

The lead Bug had some kind of military insignia attached. They wore a shimmering artificial armor, although to Jones mind, they looked difficult to kill even without it. The negotiations began:

"We will allow you to live, despite your murderous acts, because we are a charitable and benevolent society," a lead bug wrote on a large white tablet. He then uttered some unintelligible chattering sounds, which the human Autotrans could not decipher.

"If I speak, do you understand?," said Jones to the leader. It waved a tentacle towards an assistant, who wrote on the board, "Yes, we do." It pointed to a geometric assemblage that rested nearby - their translator technology.

"You will be allowed to live here, in this enclosure. If you try and escape, we will destroy you. We wish to study you. In time, we may trade together - but not for many of our cycles. You have committed grave sins against us."

"We did not know you were here. We thought this planet was unoccupied," said Jones loudly.

"You did not see evidence of our habitats?"

"We thought those had been abandoned. How were we to know. At least allow us to contact our sky ships," said Jones, pointing upward.

At that, another Bug commander waved and shook his upper arms and head-end. Their translator wrote, "No - most emphatically not. Your ships rain death on us - we cannot allow any contact. This will be your home now. Get used to it."

And before Jones could get any words out to protest, the group of Bernellians scuttled quickly back to the small opening in the barrier, and re-sealed it. The Humans were on their own.

Commander Jones looked at Science advisor Eliason, who had just returned, and grinned. "What the hell. I've always wanted to be a farmer."

"And me a teacher. Looks like we have our work cut out for us," said Eliason, shaking her blonde locks.

The human Crevice colony on Bernelli 7 began its existence behind the Barrier, one that would last for over a hundred years, until they finally discovered a way to escape. Then it was their turn to confine the Bernellians behind a similar barrier.

By Dycen Alexander

Rebound

At the thawing of the snow, oh my lad come or go.
Swim the world or drift back home, you will find me all alone.
So if think that you may wish it, come back to me and visit,
I am pacing in the garden, frosting feet in ice unhardend.
Greet me here, for neither door nor knocker can I hear
When silver crystals melt to dust, when my clockwork mind can rust,
Left to roam in this icicle waste, my melted outline can be traced.

And if you want me, I'll accept the love that you have so long kept
Inside the pinholes of your skull, shine that fire till it grows dull.
Give me this and give me that, beg for depth (although I'm flat)
I'll be your wife if you decide that you still want me by your side
And I'll be sensible, still, and wise. All will be well. Ignore my sighs.
They mean to me, alas, of foolhardy memories and times that pass
Too slowly in my peripheral vision, stinging my eyes with great precision.

My face is numb, my lips are blue with every kiss I give to you.
You reach but find only flaccid hands. You search my brain for distant lands.
Why so hurt lad? Don't complain, you're the only one who keeps me sane.
I think I mustn't fail you, for I believe your heart would break if I should leave
Like he left me, that dark-headed fool, who tossed me away, his eyes so cruel.
An innocent cruelty, he never was mine, and he does not know of how I've pined.
Oh my dark head, you've left me cold! But my lad, with you I can grow old.

In this hail-strewn bed, I can hear music strains, the velvet colors of his refrains
Of nothings of nothings of nothings that once gave me dragon wings
That beat on the mattress of this bed-- Oh those sweet lies that he once said.
But though he enters me in creeps, in your arms I remain without sleep.
I can bear your snoring drone, but even beside you, I'm still alone
To waste the night in tricks and trappings and all my hopes that he keeps sacking
With every breath and whispered wail, that dark head fills my heart with hail

Call me your darling, call me yours, tell me that your longing roars
For palpitating fires and throbbing lusts, for something gentle, for an 'us.'
My place with you is well assured and never his way will I be lured,
For he is gone like salt and song, now only for you do I belong.
And I hope someday your shining teeth will blast away this pathetic grief
But for now my lad, your joy is my desire. I'll try to be happy, but I am a liar.
So my lad, at the weeping of the snow, will you come? Or will you go?

By Ellen Webre

The Dance Most of All

Dancers lie scattered
on the wood floor, eyes closed,
stilled by a long day of movement.
Unknown fingers brush his left hand—
a question he lightly
answers. They curl together
on the floor, nurture one another
with minute movements.

He receives an email:
I often recall   three years ago
wondrous dance
do you remember
How could he forget?
They agree to meet for tea.

How could *she* not have recalled
he is her father's age? How could *he*
not have remembered how young she was,
how awkward and lost?
He drives her home, listens
as she speculates her future.
The dark streets, empty,
like a ghost town, provide
no way back.

By David Stallings

Cosmic

I re-arrange the air around me
pile it on my hands
balance it on my head
lick small drops
find the smell of starlight
leaves me wondering
is anything left on earth
to taste touch   hear?

the cat moves from floor to chair
a single hair floats onto my foot
creating an explosion
of weight upon my skin

By Joanna M. Weston

Clouds

Dawn clouds. First light tearing teasingly
at the soft, busy tongues of lovers;
at the resentful eyes of the too-early woken.

Today's rain bobbing confined, reined-in boats;
disappointed cars wait anxiously in rows.
The clouds ride on high, wisdom intact.

They go on, swallowing the sighs of dreams;
the breath of lies, the sea's sparkle.
In silent pockets they carry off our dead.

Conversations continue, cloudy apples cut and re-cut.
The houses are angry because watched from above.
On hard pavements, the poor walk under newspapers.

The clouds have seen it all, all the time;
they pass over the graves of the forgotten;
they don't whisper or cry or pass comment.

They collect until there is no sky.
Turning, a boat slips its moorings and drifts,
eyes leeward, towards the unlocking sea.

By David R Morgan

Image Of The Great War

On the Barnsley War Memorial
In front of the Town Hall,
No cross or crucifix,
No religious symbol at all.

There's a carved wreath with-
'Their names liveth for evermore' beneath.
But no religious symbol at all.
I never noticed before.

'The Barnsley Pals'
That was the regiment set up
To go to France...

To die on the Somme
For what? For Britain?
For 'Christian Civilisation'?

In front of the War Memorial
Drunken youth falling about
Flailing arms.

By James Morris

I am a Terrible Mother

I work in my garden. The trees
and the bones of trees litter my yard, and to be honest
I'm usually a little tired near the end.
And it's usually at about this time that they tell me
about their loneliness,
and how they hate themselves,
and how they hate me too.
And then they fall on the ground face down
and suffocate when dirt gets pushed over them;
and I feel really angry and I hope they rot in hell.
At the same time though,
I feel a little guilty.
There are a lot of dead bodies in my garden.

By James Medina

Bound By Plate Glass

Bound by plate glass,
Life passes
Without my knowledge,
Disengaged from my being,
As though these eyes
Were not witness,
Did not behold,
But were mere glass globes
Locked in a warm room,
The hour six,
Thursday, June.

By Richard Jay Shelton

Unemployment Benefits

You are being laid off, but
Not thrown away!
So why the sadness then,
The feeling that a death
Has happened, quite possibly
Your own?

You have the freedom now
You wanted, time to move
Towards the goals
That your ambition set up
And teased you with,
So why feel sad now?

A new life is about to start!
You do not even need
To get used to a new body,
Or take on a new name,
Yet you insist to feel hurt,
Has someone you known died?

By Ben Nardolilli

Home Videos

Filming a home video
the man farts discretely
while aiming the 8mm Sony
at his wife
eating frozen cherries
from a Super Fresh bag,
her fingertips stained
like Lucifer's
after he ripped our
hearts
from their bleeding sockets.

Drenched to her elbows
in cherry juice
the wife
exits
in her white business suit
prepared to take on Tupperware,
pharmaceutical sales,
plus the world beyond!

The cameraman
pans
the floor for dogs,
forelegs crossed,
eyes and ears twitching,
dreaming of ice-cubes,
pizza crusts
and chunks of chicken
left over
from earlier home videos.

By Alan Britt

The AMPM downtown

I have refined the "don't ask me for money" look.

After trips to Paris and Istanbul and Oxford where beggars wait for dumb Americans,

I have learned a curt headshake and frowning distant eye look that clearly says, "don't ask me."

I try not to go to the AMPM in downtown Bakersfield because

I'd rather just avoid the streetpeople or the conmen who make up convoluted stories about why I should give them my money.

And who treat me like I'm cheap if I give them less than a five.

"I just need enough gas money to make it to Riverside where my sister has a job roofing her house for me."

"Don't you have any more? Come on, I just need a little more."

But sometimes gas is cheaper there and it's more convenient to stop there, so I go.

And there is this young man who looks scruffy and unkempt and perfectly healthy enough to get a job

and I see him approaching out of the corner of my eye as he mumbles something hard to understand,

"There's a motel down the street, we just need-" but I cut him off with my effective headshake and he moves on.

As I finish pumping my gas, he walks over to a young girl standing under a yellow streetlight,

with her hands on a baby stroller.

I feel a wave of bile guilt rise in my throat as he shakes his head sadly at the girl.

They walk away and they are nearly to the end of the block before I drive behind them in my car.

I open the window and hand the man a twenty.

By Sandra Rose Hughes

1985

my first time riding cross country
i rode through pennsylvania
through towns snapshots
from a springsteen song
many years later, i would live in a
springsteen town in ohio
13,000 people
with a scottish girl who had red hair and
wide hips and three kids
(we didn't know it wasn't supposed to last...)
someone told me springsteen
wanted to be a novelist
but chose to tell stories in songs
two months of cambridge, ohio
and i begged my woman, "let's move
to a big city"
she wanted her children to know there father
she chose her kids over me
and stayed in cambridge
my hungry heart roamed to california
my plan is grow old and die here

By Erren Geraud Kelly

About the Authors

Dycen Alexander has had short fiction published in various periodicals, and has been writing fiction and poetry since 2001.

Jeffrey C. Alfier's first full-length book of poems, *The Wolf Yearling*, will be published in 2012, by Pecan Grove Press. He is founder and co-editor of *San Pedro River Review.*

Amanda Anastasi is an emerging poet from Melbourne, Australia. Amanda's work has been featured on Channel 31's *Red Lobster,* 3CR radio's Spoken Word program, and she was a *Passionate Tongues* feature poet at Melbourne's Brunswick Hotel. She is the two-time winner of the Seagull Poetry Prize and is currently working on her first collection *2012 and other poems.*

Michael Berton is an educator, tai chi aficionado, traveller and percussionist. He is former poetry editor of The Cereal Vox Review. He lives in Portland, OR.

Alan Britt's recent books are *Alone with the Terrible Universe* (2011), *Greatest Hits* (2010), *Hurricane* (2010), *Vegetable Love* (2009), *Vermilion* (2006), *Infinite Days* (2003), *Amnesia Tango* (1998) and *Bodies of Lightning* (1995). Britt's work also appears in the new anthologies, *American Poets Against the War, Metropolitan Arts Press, Chicago/Athens/Dublin: 2009* and *Vapor transatlántico* (Transatlantic Steamer), a bi-lingual anthology of Latin American and North American poets, Hofstra University Press/Fondo de Cultura Económica de Mexico/Universidad Nacional Mayor de San Marcos de Peru, 2008. Alan currently teaches English/Creative Writing at Towson University and lives in Reisterstown, Maryland with his wife, daughter, two Bouviers des Flandres, one Bichon Frise and two formally feral cats. Find out more about him at:
http://spectrumofpoeticfire.com/Reader%20Directory/Alan_Britt.htm

John F. Buckley lives in Orange County, California. His work has been published in a number of places, one of which nominated him for a Pushcart Prize in 2009. His chapbook *Breach Birth* was published on Propaganda Press in March 2011.

Janet Butler has had poems recently published or forthcoming in The North Chicago Review, Assisi, Caduceus, and The Quotable. "Searching for Eden" will be published this January, Finishing Line Press, and she was recently awarded 1st and 2nd place, HM in the Bay Area Poetry Coalition's national contest for 2012. This is the third consecutive year her poems have placed.

Idris Caffrey was born in the market town of Rhayader in Mid-Wales. His latest collection "Relatively Unscathed" was published by Cinnamon Press of North Wales.

Colin W. Campbell is originally from the UK, now dividing the year between homes faraway in Sarawak and China. Publications have included professional and academic articles and a weekly column, but today it's all fun with poetry, flash fiction and short stories.

Valentina Cano is a student of classical singing who spends whatever free time either writing or reading. Her works have appeared in *Exercise Bowler, Blinking Cursor, Theory Train, Magnolia's Press, Cartier Street Press, Berg Gasse 19, Precious Metals* and will appear in the upcoming editions of *A Handful of Dust, The Scarlet Sound, The Adroit Journal, Perceptions Literary Magazine, Welcome to Wherever, The Corner Club Press, Death Rattle, Danse Macabre, Subliminal Interiors, Generations Literary Journal, Super Poetry Highway, Stream Press, Stone Telling, Popshot* and *Perhaps I'm Wrong About the World.* You can find her at: http://coldbloodedlives.blogspot.com

S. R. Christian resides in the prairies of Canada with his dog, known to some as Ghost Wolf.

Tobi Cogswell is a two-time Pushcart nominee. Her latest chapbook is "*Surface Effects in Winter Wind*", (Kindred Spirit Press). She is the co-editor of San Pedro River Review (www.sprreview.com).

Samuel Diaz was born and raised in New York City. He is currently studying Creative Writing at the University of Chicago.

Kristina England resides in Worcester, MA. Her poetry is forthcoming or published in *Breadcrumb Scabs, Diverse Voices Quarterly, Gargoyle, Haggard and Halloo*, and other magazines.

Ruth Gooley, a native of Venice, California, published her dissertation, "The Image of the Kiss in French Renaissance Poetry", and has published poems in *Pure Francis, Poecology, The Red Poppy Review, vox poetica, nibble, Common Sense 2, The Corner Club Press, Apollo's Lyre, Ibbetson Street Press*, and *Hobble Creek Review*. She has forthcoming poems in *Snowy Egret, Literary Fever*, and *Up the Staircase*, among others.

Alan D Harris writes his stories and poetry based primarily upon the historical fictions of family and loved ones. Most recently he has been published in the 2011 summer edition of *Candidum*, Australia's 2011 *Chimaera*, UK's August 2011 *Welcometowherever* and the September 2011 edition of *Healthy Artists*. Harris has received the 2011 Stephen H Tudor Scholarship in Creative Writing from Wayne State University.

William D. Hicks is a writer who lives in Chicago, Illinois by himself (any offers?). Contrary to popular belief, he is not related to the famous comedian Bill Hicks (though he's just as funny in his own right). Hicks will someday publish his memoirs, but most likely they will be about Bill Hicks' life. His poetry has appeared in *Christmas Ideals Magazine, Outburst Magazine, The Legendary, Horizon Magazine, Breadcrumb Sins, Inwood Indiana Literary Magazine, The Short Humour Site (UK), The Four Cornered Universe, Save the Last Stall for Me* and *Mosaic*. His art appears in *The Blank Page Handbook, The Legendary* and as cover art in *Anti-Poetry*.

By day, Sandra Rose Hughes works as an English teacher in a small mountain community in California, but by night, she hovers over her computer, writing poetry, children's fiction, and short stories. Her poetry tends to be short and to the point. Sandra's poetry has been features in *Concise Delight*, *Midnight Screaming*, and the Spring 2010 edition of *Blinking Cursor*. She also keeps a humorous writing blog which chronicles her attempts at publication at:
www.mymotherthinksimagoodwriter.blogspot.com

Peycho Kanev is the Editor In Chief of Kanev Books. His poems have appeared in more than 500 literary magazines, such as: *Poetry Quarterly, The Monongahela Review, Steam Ticket, Ann Arbor Review, Midwest Literary Review, Third Wednesday, The Cleveland Review, Istanbul Literary Review, Loch Raven Review, In Posse Review, The Penwood Review, Mascara Literary Review, The Mayo Review* and many others. He is nominated for the Pushcart Award and lives in Chicago. In 2009 his short story collection *Walking Through Walls* and in April 2010 his poetry collection *American Notebooks* both were published in Bulgaria. His poetry collection *Bone Silence* was released in September 2010 by Desperanto, NY. A new collection of his poetry, *titled Limestone Memories*, will be published by Desperanto in 2012.

Erren Geraud Kelly is a poet based in New York City, by way of Louisiana, by way of Maine, by way of California and so on. Erren has been writing for 21 years and have over three dozen publications in print and online in such publications as *Hiram Poetry Review, Mudfish, Poetry Magazine* (online) and other publications. His most recent publication was in *In Our Own Words*, a Generation X poetry anthology; He was also published in other anthologies such as *Fertile Ground*, *Beyond The Frontier* and other anthologies.

Steve Klepetar teaches literature and writing at Saint Cloud State University in Minnesota. His work has received several nominations for the Pushcart Prize and Best of the Net.

Jerry Kraft is a playwright, poet and theatre critic in Port Angeles, Washington. His plays have been widely produced, his poetry has appeared in many journals and his reviews appear regularly on www.SeattleActor.com. He believes in beautiful language, the expression of genuine experience and the drama of human interaction. He always promises to try writing something better tomorrow.

Karlanna Lewis has recently completed her honors B.A. at Florida State University in Russian and Creative Writing, with an honors thesis in poetry. Her writing has also been published in numerous journals and received various awards including winning the 2011 Phi Kappa Phi Forum Poetry Contest. She has also been writer-in-residence at artist studios such as Elsewhere Studios in Colorado, and has been offered a writer-in-residence position at Camac Art Centre in France in 2012. In addition, she dances with a small Tallahassee company, Pas de Vie Ballet, and hopes to work in the field of the arts all her life.

Mercedes Lucero is currently a senior at Missouri Western State University. She has previously been published in *North Central Review* and *Canvas.*

James Medina is a California writer and a graduate of Literature and Creative Writing at California State University Northridge. He's had his work published in their literary journal and adores playing with literary structure and format. James revels in old books, mythology, and the superstition of everyday life, he is wary of the Fair Folk, the Minotaur, and traffic wardens. This is his first published piece in *Blinking Cursor*.

Sonnet Mondal has authored seven full length books of poetry published by renowned Indian publishers like *Authorspress*, New Delhi and *Sparrow Publication*, Kolkata. He was bestowed *Poet Laureate* from *Bombadil Publishing,* Sweden in 2009. His works have appeared in more than hundred international literary publications. He was inducted in the prestigious *Significant Achievements Plaque* at the museum of *Bengal Engineering and Science University*, Shibpur in 2011, nominated for *Pushcart Prize* in 2011 and was featured as one of the *Famous Five of Bengali youths* by *India Today* magazine in 2010. At present he is the managing editor of *The Enchanting Verses Literary Review,* Editor of *Best Poems Encyclopedia, Editor of Sonnets in the New Millenium (to be released from Diamond Point Press, U.S.A.)* and the Sub Secretary General of *Poetas Del Mundo.*

David R Morgan teaches 11-19 year olds in Luton, and lives in Bedfordshire. He has been an arts worker and literature officer, organizer of book festivals and writer-in-residence for education authorities, Littlehay Prison and Fairfield Psychiatric Hospital (which was the subject of a Channel 4 film, Out of Our Minds).He has had two plays screened on ITV and over 200 hundred poems published in National and International Poetry Magazines. David has also written poetry books, including: *The Broken Picture Book*, The *Windmill and the Grains* (Hawthorn Prize) and *Buzz Off.* His poetry collection *Walrus on a Rocking Chair*, illustrated by John Welding, is published by *Claire Publications* and his last adult poetry *Ticket for the Peepshow* was published by *art'icle international.*

James Morris has had two poems published in *The Spectator*. He has on-going publication of his 'Waugh Poems' in the *Evelyn Waugh Newsletter,* and on-going publication of his 'Chesterton Poems' in *The Chesterton Review.* James come from Barnsley, South Yorkshire and his favourite poet is Ernest Dowson.

Ben Nardolilli currently lives in Arlington, Virginia. His work has appeared in *Perigee Magazine, Red Fez, One Ghana One Voice, Caper Literary Journal, Quail Bell Magazine, Elimae, Super Arrow, Grey Sparrow Journal, Pear Noir, Rabbit Catastrophe Review*, and *Yes Poetry*. His chapbook *Common Symptoms of an Enduring Chill Explained*, has been published by Folded Word Press. He maintains a blog at mirrorsponge.blogspot.com and is looking to publish his first novel.

Douglas Polk is a writer of poetry from central Nebraska. Feeling persecuted most of his life he has published three books of poetry; *In My Defense, The Defense Rests*, and *On Appeal*. He lives with his wife and two boys and two dogs on the plains of Nebraska.

Ruth Sabath Rosenthal is a New York (U.S.A.) poet. Her poems have been published in numerous literary journals and poetry anthologies in the U.S. and abroad. In 2006, her poem "on yet another birthday" was nominated for a Pushcart prize. Ruth's debut chapbook "Facing Home," published by Finishing Line Press, can be purchased from amazon.com USA: ISBN 9781599246321; and her full-length book of poetry titled "Facing Home and Beyond," published by Paragon Poetry Press, can also be purchased from amazon.com USA: ISBN 9780692013236, and from the publisher: paragonpoetry@aol.com. For more about Ruth, visit www.ruthsabathrosenthal.moonfruit.com

Gonzalo Salesky is an Argentine poet and short story writer. He was born on 12th December 1978 in Córdoba, Argentina. So far, he has published two books, *2011* (poems and short stories) in 2009 and *Presagio de Luz* ("Harbinger of Light", poems) in 2010. These books can be downloaded from his blog at http://gonzalosalesky.blogspot.com. He has been awarded several prizes in literary contests in the USA, Spain, Mexico, Venezuela and Argentina.

Richard Jay Shelton was born in 1946 on a navy base in Coronado, California, but has lived most of his life in Los Angeles. He has been writing and painting for forty-five years. His paintings can be found in the Smithsonian Institution, among other museums. The poems selected are part of three larger works titled, "Carefully Chosen Words", and "Pathetic Poetics".

Fiona Sinclair's work has been published in numerous magazines. Her collection *A game of Hide and Seek* will be published by Indigo Dreams Press. She is the editor of the on line poetry magazine *Message in a Bottle.*

David Stallings was born in the U.S. South, raised in Alaska and Colorado before settling in the Pacific Northwest. Once an academic geographer, he has spent many years promoting public transportation in the Puget Sound area. His poems have appeared in several North American and U.K. literary journals and anthologies.

Michael N. Thompson is the author of *Dancing Inside The Mouth Of Madness* and *This Hollow Pierces.* He has also been published in various literary journals. After barely surviving the death of hair metal, numerous riots and the occasional earthquake in Los Angeles, Michael packed up his significant other and his cats for his hometown of San Francisco where he can now cheer relentlessly for his beloved 49ers and Giants without consequence.

Anthony Ward is from the North of England and has been writing in his spare time for a number of years. He has been published in a number of literary magazines including *South, Neon Highway, Borderlines, Esssence,* and *Blinking Cursor* among others.

Ellen Webre is an aspiring writer from a writing conservatory. Her world is an international canvas of inspiration, and catalyzes her interpretation of literary works.

Joanna M. Weston has had poetry, reviews, and short stories published in anthologies and journals for twenty-five years. Her middle-reader, *Those Blue*

Shoes, published by Clarity House Press; and poetry, *A Summer Father*, published by Frontenac House of Calgary. Find out more about her at: http://1960willowtree.wordpress.com

Jan Wiezorek writes and teaches at an elementary school in Chicago. His fiction has appeared at PressboardPress.com, ShadowFictionPress.com, CommuterLit.com, Ozone Park Journal, CracktheSpine.com, *Seeds Literary Arts Journal* in Chicago, Sleepytown Press, TheWriteMag.com, AbsintheRevival.net, and Our Day's Encounter. Jan is author of *Awesome Art Projects That Spark Super Writing* (New York: Scholastic, 2011). He holds an M.A. in Interdisciplinary Arts Education from Columbia College Chicago and a B.A. in Journalism from Iowa State University. Jan also studied fiction writing at Northeastern Illinois University. He enjoys biking along the country roads in Harbor Country of southwestern Michigan.

BD Wilson is a writer from Edmonton, Alberta, Canada. A firm believer in a virtual existence, BD's home on the Web is located at www.bdwilson.ca.

Kirby Wright was a Visiting Fellow at the 2009 International Writers Conference in Hong Kong, where he represented the Pacific Rim region of Hawaii. He was also a Visiting Writer at the 2010 Martha's Vineyard Residency in Edgartown, Mass., and the 2011 Artist in Residence at Milkwood International, Czech Republic. He is the author of the companion novels *Punahou Blues* and *Moloka'i Nui Ahina*, both set in the islands.

Heather Wyatt currently works in the technical department of a marketing company in Tuscaloosa, AL. She is also a part time instructor at the University of Alabama. Her work has been published in *The Marr's Field Journal, Public Republic, Snakeskin, tak'tik* and *The Broad River Review.* She also has forthcoming poetry publications in*Stymie Magazine* and *The Whistling Fire.*

Changming Yuan, author of *Chansons of a Chinaman* and 4-time Pushcart nominee, grew up in rural China and published several monographs before moving to Canada. Currently, Yuan teaches in Vancouver. starts to edit *Poetry Pacific*, a new webzine, and has had poetry appearing in 430 literary publications across 18 countries, including *Asia Literary Review, Barrow Street, Best Canadian Poetry, BestNewPoemsOnline, Blinking Cursor, London Magazine, Orbis, Poetry Kanto, Poetry Salzburg* and *Poetry Scotland*.

Zarina Zabrisky started to write at six. She earned her MFA from St. Petersburg State University in Russia. She wrote and travelled around the world as a translator, kickboxing instructor, street artist, and a model. She is an author of a novel and a collection of short stories. Her short story appeared in *Full of Crow Quarterly Fiction*. Zarina lives in San Francisco.